MADE IN HIS IMAGE
THE CHRISTIAN AND ABORTION

MADE IN HIS IMAGE
THE CHRISTIAN AND ABORTION

Dr Philip Mullan

40 Beansburn, Kilmarnock, Scotland

ISBN-13: 978 1 914273 13 1

Copyright © 2021 by John Ritchie Ltd.
40 Beansburn, Kilmarnock, Scotland

www.ritchiechristianmedia.co.uk

All rights reserved. No part of this publication may be reproduced, stored in a retrievable system, or transmitted in any form or by any other means – electronic, mechanical, photocopy, recording or otherwise – without prior permission of the copyright owner.

Typeset by John Ritchie Ltd., Kilmarnock
Printed by 4edge Ltd., Essex

CONTENTS

Introduction 7

1. The Wonder of Life 9

2. The Value of Human Life 15

3. At What Point Does Human Life Begin? 25

4. The Reality of Abortion 31

5. Alternatives to Abortion: Responding with Love 39

    a) Caring for the unborn 39

    b) Caring for the mothers involved 42

    c) Caring in extremely difficult circumstances 44

    d) Caring for the unwanted 46

    e) Caring for the unexpected 49

Endnotes and References 51

MADE IN HIS IMAGE

INTRODUCTION

The abortion debate raises sensitive issues and often provokes strong reactions on both sides of the argument. As we consider the Bible's teaching on this matter, it is vital that we do not simply discuss things in a theoretical way, but also consider the real heartache, distress and fear that many women and couples face. As we progress through this little book I want us to think carefully of ways in which we can genuinely support them.

A lot of people say that abortion is a woman's issue, and that, as a man, I should not speak about it. But, as a Christian, I believe God has spoken about it, and His voice must be heard. We must be willing to submit to His truth, knowing that He is good, and His ways are best. What I have written is what I believe the Bible teaches on this issue. Through my work as a GP I have met many women with unplanned pregnancies. I have always tried to treat them with care and compassion, whether they decided to keep the baby or not, because the Bible teaches that all are valuable in God's sight – the unborn child, the single teenage mum, and those who have had abortions. It is vital then that on this contentious issue we speak the truth in love (Ephesians 4:15), and thus remind people of our Lord Jesus Christ, the one who was *"full of grace and truth"* (John 1:14).

I want to thank my wonderful wife Esther, as well as Paul McCauley and Fraser Munro for all their help with editing.

Psalm 139:13-18

You formed my inward parts;
You covered me in my mother's womb.
I will praise You, for I am fearfully and wonderfully made;
Marvellous are Your works,
And that my soul knows very well.
My frame was not hidden from You,
When I was made in secret,
And skillfully wrought in the lowest parts of the earth.
Your eyes saw my substance, being yet unformed.
And in Your book they all were written,
The days fashioned for me,
When as yet there were none of them.
How precious also are Your thoughts to me, O God!
How great is the sum of them!
If I should count them, they would be more in number than the sand.

CHAPTER 1
THE WONDER OF LIFE

> *"I will praise You, for I am fearfully and wonderfully made; marvellous are Your works, and that my soul knows very well."* **Psalm 139:14**

It is a privilege to be alive. How grateful we should be that we were given the opportunity to live. It is easy to take our existence for granted, as well as the reality that we can think, feel and communicate. But have you ever stopped to consider the fact that you are here? What a wonder it is that we have thoughts in our head, breath in our lungs, and life in our blood!

The wonder of our soul and its consciousness

Each of us is made up of a body, soul and spirit (1 Thessalonians 5:23). We are unique people with our own stories, hopes and dreams. Yet the consciousness we possess and enjoy is not merely the product of our physical brains, as some would claim. Our actions are not simply the result of chemicals in our brain reacting to the body's surroundings. Each of us is a conscious, immaterial soul (Matthew 10:28) with a mind and a will that interacts with our body through our brain. Only God knows how this fusion of spiritual and physical occurs. Truly we are *"fearfully and wonderfully made."*

Being souls, we all have the ability to learn and to reason. We can grapple with both practical and ethical problems. Each of us has a conscience and can tell right from wrong. We are a melting pot of emotions. Who does not love the thrill of a breath-taking view or a fantastic piece of music? Or the fun, companionship and emotional connection that close relationships bring? What a joy it is to know and be known.

The wonder of our body and its complexity

In the verses quoted above, the ancient poet King David praises God for being wonderfully made. Although it was 1000 BC, David understood something of the immense complexity that makes us who we are. As scientific understanding of the body and its development has advanced, David's statement has proven to be so appropriate: *"I am fearfully and wonderfully made."* We now know the body is full of ingeniously designed organs, cells and microstructures. Let us briefly consider the amazing journey of human development.

From the moment of conception all the information needed to make us who we are is present in 46 supercoiled strands of DNA called chromosomes. That one little cell soon begins to multiply, differentiating into many different types of cells and tissues. Each cell knows its role and behaves with purpose and precision.

Just five or six days after conception the microscopic ball of human cells burrows into the lining of the womb and begins the process of implantation. This alters the mother's hormones and prevents the pregnancy being rejected. 18 days after conception the first elements of the nervous system begin to form and by day 22 or 23 the embryonic heart begins to beat. During the following nine weeks the rest of the baby's organs are formed.

> **What is clear is that each human body bears the marks of intricate engineering and design."**

It astounds me that by week 12 of pregnancy the baby has all of the structures required for life both inside and outside the womb. For example, while the baby is inside the womb, small holes in the heart allow blood to bypass the lungs and flow to the placenta. The lungs are not needed at this point but they develop nonetheless. However as soon as the baby is born and takes its first breath, blood is diverted into the lungs to start absorbing oxygen, and the holes in its heart begin to close. Our circulatory system has been perfectly designed so that at birth it transforms, enabling life to continue in the outside world.

I remember the day our first child was born. As the scrawny little bundle was lifted to my wife for the first time, we didn't need to teach him how to feed. He did it instinctively. Each of us was born with this built-in suck reflex. I would have no idea how to get a newborn to suck and swallow milk if it didn't know how. Thankfully, that is the way we are made. Such a reflex could not evolve: prior to the advent of modern medicine if a baby could not suck it died. It is yet another reminder of the fact that we have been specially created by God. We are not an accidental product of evolution.

I have only touched on a few of the wonders of the human body and its development. Much more could be said about the intricacies of how nerves function, how we filter waste chemicals in the kidneys, the complexities of the retina and binocular vision, as well as the memory of the immune system, but this is not the place to do so. What is clear is that each human body bears the marks of intricate engineering and design.

Considering our bodies and the gift of life should cause us to marvel. Each organ, and each cell, has been wonderfully made.

But when King David wrote the words of Psalm 139:14, he was saying more than that. He saw within us evidence of our Creator. We are God's creation. We are His bespoke masterpieces. The design of our cells, organs and body systems, as well as the ingenuity and precision of all of the processes going on within our bodies should cause us to bow in awe before the living God. That is the idea of being *"fearfully"* made by God. What He has made is awe inspiring, and for this He deserves our adoration.

The wonder of a spiritual relationship with our Creator

David commences the verse with the words, *"I will praise You."* This is perhaps the greatest thing about human life. We have been made for relationship with God. We can worship the Creator of the universe. More than that, we can come to know Him for we are spirit as well as body. *"God is Spirit, and those who worship Him must worship in spirit and truth"* (John 4:24). God created humans for relationship with Him, and initially God and man walked together in harmony (Genesis 3:8). Sin ruined this. By turning away from God, mankind is missing out on what we were made for. Many fail to benefit from this wonderful aspect of human life, for they will not repent of their sins and place their faith in Christ to save them. They do not know forgiveness of sins. God wants to bring us back into close relationship with Him, and promises eternal life to all who will accept His Son as Saviour. *"This is eternal life, that they may know You, the only true God, and Jesus Christ whom You have sent"* (John 17:3).

As we consider the abortion debate and the value of human life it is vital that we remember that we are God's creatures and it is best that we listen to what He says on the matter. Our Creator has given us guidance for life in the Bible, and we would do well to follow it. Psalm 119:105 states; *"Your word is a lamp to my feet and a light to my path."*

We have seen how amazing it is to be alive. Life is a blessing to be valued and enjoyed (James 1:17). We are deeply complex beings, and every part of us bears the fingerprints of our great Creator God. Whether we consider our soul and its emotions and intellect, our body and the irreducible complexity it contains, or our spirit and the possibility of relationship with our Maker, we come to the same conclusion: *"we are fearfully and wonderfully made."*

This is the life we are going to be considering in this booklet, which in many cases is cut short by abortion. In the next chapter we will consider why human life is so valuable, and how this impacts our decisions in relation to abortion.

MADE IN HIS IMAGE

CHAPTER 2
THE VALUE OF HUMAN LIFE

On 10th December 1948, at the third session of the United Nations General Assembly held in Paris, the Universal Declaration of Human Rights was signed. It was three years since the Second World War had ended and, with it, the horrors of the Holocaust. Approximately 70 to 85 million people died during the war, with around 6 million Jews being exterminated throughout Europe by the Nazis. In response to the shocking accounts of torture and suffering that surfaced after the war, the United Nations Universal Declaration of Human Rights emphasised "the inherent dignity" and "the equal and inalienable rights of all members of the human family." The Declaration stated, "All humans are born free and equal in dignity and rights ... Everyone has the right to life, liberty and security of person." This declaration formed the basis for the European Convention of Human Rights and the Human Rights Act 1998 (UK) which both state, "No one shall be deprived of his life intentionally."

These human rights continue to be widely accepted, and we often take them for granted. Yet the foundation that these rights are based on is often poorly understood. It is in fact biblical teaching on the value of life that provides the basis for claiming that all are equal. Indeed, the Bible goes further than the human rights declarations I have mentioned, for it includes the unborn.

In this chapter I want to consider six biblical reasons why every human, born and unborn, has value and deserves life.

a) We are made in the image of God

> *"Then God said, "Let Us make man in Our image, according to Our likeness ... So God created man in His own image ... male and female He created them."* **Genesis 1:26, 27**

Human life is special and unique because we are made in God's image and according to His likeness. We are more than mere animals. All of us, both males and females, bear something of God's qualities. This is not referring to how we appear physically, but rather that each of us display some of His characteristics.

Being made in the image of God has three consequences.

1. We are able to have a relationship with God.

God made humans after His likeness so He could dwell with them and have relationship with them. It is God's desire that He should know us and we Him (John 17:3, Revelation 21:3). In the early chapters of Genesis, before man's rebellion, God spoke with man (1:28-30, 2:16-17), brought the animals to him for naming (2:19) and conducted the first marriage between Adam and Eve (2:22). In Genesis 3:8, God walked in the garden in the cool of the day and it seems that this was what He often did. This closeness of relationship is what God originally intended, and it was our sin and rebellion as a human race that ruined it. Thankfully this can be restored through repentance and faith in the Lord Jesus.

Without God's likeness we would not have the ability to communicate with God, nor the awareness to worship Him. Animals are unaware of their Maker and are unable to have a relationship with Him. We stand unique from the rest of the physical creation. We have been made *"for Him"* (Colossians 1:16).

2. We will be held responsible as representatives of God.

When God created mankind He gave us dominion over the rest of creation to act as His agents in caring for and managing the world (Genesis 1:26; 2:15, Psalm 8:6). God therefore expects us to behave in a manner that is in keeping with His character and which displays His wonderful attributes. He wants us to be good, kind, honest and trustworthy.

God has placed limits on what we can and cannot do (Genesis 2:17, Exodus 20:1-17), which includes not just our treatment of nature, but also how we treat Him as well as others. The God who made us will one day be our judge. Each of us will *"give account of himself to God"* (Romans 14:12). Being an image-bearer brings responsibility as to how we act.

3. We have inherent value.

Our value as individuals does not rest on what we can do, or what we have attained. We are valuable because we are image-bearers of the Living God. Just as the image of the Queen on a pound coin conveys value to an otherwise worthless piece of metal, so being created in God's likeness conveys value to us. As we have learnt, we are made by Him and for Him. He loves us and wants a relationship with us. God has a purpose for each individual's life.

In Job 31:13-15, Job describes how the value of master and servant did not rest on their status and wealth, or lack of it, but on what they were as creatures of God. He highlights the fact that there are no distinctions in the womb: *"Did not He who made me in the womb make them?"* Regardless of job, wealth, intelligence, success, gender, nationality or skin colour, we are all creatures made in God's image, and are all of great value to Him. The unborn embryo and the terminally ill patient are of as much value as the successful businessman or the famous celebrity. No human life is to be discarded as cheap and meaningless. It all belongs to God. It has His mark on it.

b) We each have an eternal soul

> *"And the Lord God formed man of the dust of the ground, and breathed into his nostrils the breath of life; and man became a living soul."* **Genesis 2:7 (KJV)**

When God made Adam a living soul, it was then that he became a conscious, eternal being with a mind, a will and emotions. Every human since Adam is a living soul too. Although billions have died and left behind all they lived for, their souls live on. The success and wealth a person gains in life is only temporary (1 Timothy 6:7) and adds nothing to an individual's intrinsic worth. Whether we are rich or poor, strong or weak, born or unborn, we are eternal souls and that makes us valuable.

In Matthew 16:26 we hear the Lord Jesus asking an important question, *"What profit is it to a man if he gains the whole world, and loses his own soul? Or what will a man give in exchange for his soul?"* This reminds us that there can be nothing more valuable than a soul. You could be the richest person in the world, and yet to lose your soul in hell would be the most terrible tragedy. The entire world's wealth would not compensate for such a loss, for every soul is priceless.

The fact that we are eternal souls means that our actions toward each other have eternal consequences. Those who have wronged us will one day receive the justice they deserve when

God sits in judgment. (Romans 12:19 *"'Vengeance is Mine, I will repay,' says the Lord."*) But the wrongs we have inflicted on others will also be judged if we have not repented of them and trusted Christ for salvation. In God's eyes each human life has infinite value and He expects us to treat one another in light of what we are worth to Him. This includes unborn babies.

c) God values every child

> *"But Jesus said, 'Let the little children come to Me, and do not forbid them; for of such is the kingdom of heaven.'"* **Matthew 19:14**

Little children matter to God. When the Lord Jesus lived on earth He welcomed young children and *"took them up in His arms"* (Mark 10:16). His disciples thought of children as an inconvenience and a distraction from the things that really mattered, rebuking those who brought them to see Jesus. But the Lord was displeased with the disciples' attitude. He taught that children should be individually welcomed and valued, not cast aside.

For some in our society, children are seen as an inconvenience: getting in the way and potentially derailing their career. Indeed, some celebrate abortion as being essential to fulfilling one's potential.[1] It is considered needful to "protect" women from the "misfortune" of pregnancy and motherhood. This way of thinking is foreign to the Bible. In Psalm 127:3-5 the writer contemplates the great blessing that children are.

> *"Behold, children are a heritage from the Lord,*
> *The fruit of the womb is a reward.*
> *Like arrows in the hand of a warrior,*
> *So are the children of one's youth.*
> *Happy is the man who has his quiver full of them;*

> *They shall not be ashamed,*
> *But shall speak with their enemies in the gate."*

Children are to be celebrated. Each young life is full of potential and it is our privilege as parents to direct and shape their lives to be something for God. Of course many days are difficult. Potty training and cleaning up when they are sick will never be glamorous. But each day spent with them is a valuable investment into the long-term project that is childrearing. The prospect of being able to have children should be met with joy, not embarrassment or self-pity.

Of course, there are couples that are unable to have children for health reasons and we must acknowledge their heartache and disappointment. This is a whole different issue that has been covered by many elsewhere, but it is important for us to note that infertility is not a sign of God's displeasure or of personal sin. Often it is simply the result of living in a fallen world with imperfect bodies. Too many thoughtless comments have been made to these hurting couples. We must be loving and sensitive when discussing the subject of having children.

Children should not be taken for granted. If we are blessed with having our own, we are to count them as an inheritance gift from the Lord. That is the idea of the word "*heritage*." If we, with God's help and grace, invest in their lives while they are young, when they are grown we will reap the benefits. We therefore should value the children God has given us, whether born or unborn, and invest our time, energy, prayers and money into their upbringing.

d) God feels the pain of every death

> *"When Jesus saw her weeping, and the Jews who had come with her also weeping, he was deeply moved in his spirit and greatly troubled ... Jesus wept."* **John 11:33,35 (ESV)**

Further demonstration of how God values life is seen when we consider how the Lord Jesus reacted to His friend Lazarus' death. Death greatly troubled Him, and affected Him to the core of His being. The Greek word *'enebrimesato'* that the apostle John uses here is a very strong word and carries with it the sense of anger. For this reason the Holman Christian Standard Bible translates the verse, *"He was angry in His spirit and deeply moved."* The New Living Translation goes further, *"a deep anger welled up within him, and he was deeply troubled."*

The loss of human life is not a little thing for God. It deeply moves Him. He loves us, and each death is a reminder of the sad results of man's rebellion against Him. This was not how He created the world to be.

Jesus wept. Both those who have died and those who mourn are dear to Him. His love extends even to the vilest criminal and the most blasphemous atheist. Ezekiel 33:11 is clear; *"I have no pleasure in the death of the wicked, but that the wicked turn from his way and live."* When we consider this, how must God feel when He sees innocent babies being killed?

e) God paid an immeasurable price to provide salvation for all

> *"You were not redeemed with corruptible things, like silver or gold ... but with the precious blood of Christ."* **1 Peter 1:18,19**

If you have ever had to buy life insurance you may have noticed how much insurance companies are willing to pay out if you take ill. They will provide hundreds of thousands of pounds if needed. It seems a tremendous amount of money to spend on one person, yet the payout does have a limit. A person's medical care costs may exceed the insurance company's maximum limit

"... God sets a much higher value on human life."

and, despite the person's great need, the insurance company can refuse to pay any more. In essence they are saying, "You are not worth it."

In the Bible we find that God sets a much higher value on human life. This is not a monetary value, for no amount of money could equal the value of an eternal soul. Rather our value is seen in the precious blood of Christ that flowed down the cross at Calvary. The fact that God *"did not spare His own Son, but delivered Him up for us all"* (Romans 8:32) proves that, despite our rebellion and sinfulness, we are as valuable to God as His dear Son (see also John 17:23). He was prepared to give up His perfect, dearly loved Son for us.

God values each of us so much that He reckoned this costly sacrifice to be worthwhile in order to make salvation available for everyone. *"For God so loved the world that He gave His only begotten Son, that whoever believes in Him should not perish but have everlasting life"* (John 3:16). Christ's death is indisputable evidence of our immeasurable value.

f) God has clearly forbidden murder
- *"You shall not murder."* **Exodus 20:13**

The 10 commandments are a summary of God's moral standards. The sixth command is relevant to our consideration of the value of life. God states: *"You shall not murder."* Taking an innocent life is breaking God's law. It is not something we as humans should ever contemplate, no matter how frail or how small the individual is. Regardless of what benefits one could gain from an abortion or the inconvenience it might avoid, the scripture is clear that murder is wrong.

Aborting an unborn child is not an amoral act. Medical professionals may suggest abortion is the best way forward, or set it forth as an equally 'viable' option to continuing the pregnancy. Yet abortion is a deliberate termination of innocent human life. A couple of tablets may seem incomparable to a gun or a knife, but their effect is the same. God values everyone and His law is clear: murder is forbidden.

In Genesis 9:5-6 God permits capital punishment for those guilty of murder. Human life is of such value in God's sight, that to take it from another means forfeiting the right to our own. If the victim is dead, what right has the perpetrator to live? Of course we know this is not the law of our land, and I am certainly not advocating taking the law into our own hands! But the passage emphasises an important point. Murder is a crime of the greatest severity.

We should remember that women who have had abortions often have been pressurised, or may not have been given a true choice.[2] There are often a number of other people at least partly responsible for the decision. Many women are left with guilt about what has happened, and although they usually bear the ultimate responsibility for their actions, they deserve our compassion and kindness. The Christian response should be to love and care for these broken-hearted souls. God's heart is one that offers forgiveness to all. There is cleansing of sin and freedom from guilt available through faith in the Lord Jesus. We as Christians must demonstrate this same attitude, remembering that we too have broken God's law and were once hopelessly lost.

Nevertheless, the fact remains that abortion ends another's life, and as such it breaks God's clear command not to kill.

MADE IN HIS IMAGE

CHAPTER 3
AT WHAT POINT DOES HUMAN LIFE BEGIN?

The crux of the abortion debate hinges on the question of when human life begins. Nearly everyone would agree that murder is wrong and would protest wildly at the thought of someone killing a newborn baby. Yet many people soothe their conscience in relation to abortion by telling themselves that the aborted baby is still "the mother's body." She has the right to choose what happens to her own body. It is argued that the "products of conception" are only a clump of human cells and not an actual person.

For example, Professor Cecili Chadwick (Professor in Women's Studies, California State University, San Marcos) explained in an abortion debate in 2010, "to be pro-choice is to believe that the foetus and the woman are one person: that one person is the woman." She expanded on this by saying, "The woman is carrying a potential child with potential rights."[3] The argument goes that if the unborn child is not a person, then it has no actual rights and there is nothing wrong with discarding it. Abortion is therefore deemed by its advocates to be "the least bad of several bad courses of action."[4] If, however, human life begins at the moment of conception, the foetus is in fact a separate entity and these arguments do not hold water. No matter what size or stage of development the unborn child is at, it has the right to life.

Therefore we need to ask ourselves the question, "At what point does human life begin?" The answer will tell us whether abortion is murder or medicine.

a) What does science tell us?

When a mother's egg cell is fertilised by a sperm cell something completely new is formed. Genetic material from the father is joined with genetic material from the mother creating a truly unique being. It is neither its mother nor its father, but a new human. If you could investigate every family on earth, and test every individual throughout the pages of history, not one would be found with the same genome as that little cell of human life. From the moment of conception the baby's sex and other personal characteristics (such as hair and eye colour) are determined, being encoded in his or her DNA. The mystery of conception is that the newly fertilised egg carries the same life as its mother and father yet is completely different from them. It is something new that has never existed before.

It is important to realise that the unique, personally identifiable code of DNA that the baby will carry for the rest of its life is present from the moment of conception. No further genetic material will be added later to make it more human. The "instruction manual" for growing a heart, for developing a brain, and for making the unborn child all that he or she will be, is present the moment that very first cell is conceived. And although it is only one cell, it is an amazingly complex living organism that will soon begin multiplying. A fascinating array of mechanisms exists in that one cell and works with precision to correctly 'copy and paste' the new genome and then divide the cell in two. It will then continue to divide further to form a small ball of cells (a blastocyst). When implantation occurs the embryonic baby will need a good blood supply and some of its cells form the placenta, allowing the baby to get the nutrients it needs from its mother. By week 12 all the essential body organs have begun to grow, yet nothing in this amazing process adds a single fragment of genetic information to this little individual.

Taking this information into consideration, the only logical point at which human life begins is the moment of conception. The fertilised egg is genetically distinct from both mother and father yet genetically complete; possessing all the information it needs to grow into an adult. To decide that life or "the person" starts at a later stage of development is quite an arbitrary decision to make, for which there is no concrete basis. Those who make this argument seem to do so for ideological rather than scientific reasons, allowing them to promote abortion as a morally acceptable procedure.

In the previous chapter we considered the value of human life and the biblical basis for human rights. We saw that every human is of immeasurable worth in God's eyes. What they can or cannot do does not change what they are: individuals made in God's image. Human rights legislation is clear that a person's disability does not make them any less human. Why then should the fact that an unborn baby is completely dependent on its mother cause us to think it is not a unique human being? It does not make sense that the short journey from inside the womb to the outside world should change the act of killing a baby from being morally acceptable to being morally abhorrent.

I find it baffling that doctors will work night and day to save the life of a 24-weeker in neonatal intensive care, while in the same hospital a similarly-aged baby may be deliberately terminated. The ethical reasoning that approves such different outcomes is seriously flawed. In effect it is claiming that a baby is only a human being if it is wanted. If we were to apply this logic to the rest of life the results would be unthinkable. We cannot deny the scientific facts. There is no reason to believe that human life begins at any point other than conception.

b) What does the Bible say?

The Bible is clear that unborn babies are human beings. According to scripture life does not begin at birth. In Psalm 139:15-16 David writes about God's knowledge of him even while in the womb.

> *"My frame was not hidden from You,*
> *When I was made in secret,*
> *And skillfully wrought in the lowest parts of the earth.*
> *Your eyes saw my substance, being yet unformed."*

During this time he was not his mother's body, or a mere clump of cells, but a person known by God. Being a developing foetus in the womb did not make him any less of a person, or any less human. God saw him and was aware of his existence even before he had all his body parts. The Hebrew word for "skillfully wrought" can also mean 'embroidered.' As a little embryo David was delicately and deliberately made. We can apply this to all unborn children. Every embryo is seen and known of God. Each is an individual person. They are developing human beings. But they are not developing into human beings.

David again writes in Psalm 51:5, *"Behold, I was brought forth in iniquity, and in sin my mother conceived me."* As David writes about his beginning, he goes to the moment of conception. He is clear that it was he who had been there ever since conception: *"My mother"* conceived *"me."* David's main point in this psalm is the need for repentance. David realises that he is by nature a sinner, and that he has been at a distance from God from his first moment of existence – conception. That is why he turns to God and pleads for mercy and cleansing. The same can be said for each of us. From the moment of conception we are sinners in need of a Saviour.

A number of other scriptures support the concept of unborn babies having life and being full people. In Job 10:18,19 Job laments the day of his birth because of the many tragedies he had suffered. He wishes he had died in the womb and states, *"I would have been as though I had not been. I would have been carried from the womb to the grave."* We should note the words *"as though I had not been."* If he had died in the womb he still would have existed. Yet to the outside world it would have seemed as if he hadn't. Many do not consider miscarried or aborted babies to be individuals, but this passage makes it clear that in God's sight they are.

A number of Bible characters were called from their *"mother's womb."* In Jeremiah 1:5 God tells Jeremiah, *"Before I formed you in the womb I knew you; Before you were born I sanctified you; I ordained you a prophet to the nations."* Samson could say of himself, *"I have been a Nazarite to God from my mother's womb"* (Judges 16:17). Paul wrote to the Galatians, *"It pleased God, who separated me from my mother's womb and called me through His grace, to reveal His Son in me"* (Galatians 1:15,16). These passages remind us that God has a plan and purpose for every unborn child. Each little baby, even in the womb, has so much potential for God. To abort an embryo is to end the life of one for whom God has great plans.

The Bible is clear that unborn children are human beings as much as infants and adults. Each one is a miraculous fusion of body, soul and spirit. From the moment of conception they are individuals intimately known and loved by God.

MADE IN HIS IMAGE

CHAPTER 4
THE REALITY OF ABORTION

It is estimated that 25% of all pregnancies end in an abortion. Data from the World Health Organisation shows that between 2010 and 2014 this totalled an average of 56 million abortions in the world each year.[5] These are truly sobering statistics. However, the reality is that widespread acceptance does not make abortion morally acceptable.

All would agree that abortion is a sensitive subject. Any woman who has had an abortion would probably prefer if she had never had to be in that position. It is an emotional decision, often in difficult circumstances. Some women face pressure from family members or friends to end their pregnancy. In certain circumstances health professionals have been known to strongly encourage their patients to have an abortion. Alternatives to abortion are rarely discussed as valid options. These are just a few of the many reasons women choose to abort their unborn child. The result for the woman involved is often guilt and regret lingering for many years.

As we begin considering what abortion actually is, my aim is not to make anyone feel guilty. I simply want us all to know the reality of what we are discussing. Often when advice is given to women in relation to abortion the language chosen is deliberately vague. For example, in their patient information leaflet on abortion care, the Royal College of Obstetricians and Gynaecologists refer to the unborn child as the "pregnancy tissue," or the "contents of the uterus."[6] In doing so they hide the reality that the unborn child is a person, and so minimise what an abortion is.

It is possible that someone reading this has had an abortion. Perhaps you have been plagued with guilt because of it. The good news is that there is forgiveness available for all who will come to Christ in repentance and faith. 1 John 1:7 states, *"The blood of Jesus Christ His Son cleanses us from all sin."* Hebrews 8:12 contains a wonderful promise to all who believe: *"Their sins and their lawless deeds I will remember no more."*

Who can have an abortion?

Abortions in England, Scotland and Wales are carried out in accordance with the Abortion Act 1967. In Northern Ireland abortion law has very recently been changed, and The Abortion (Northern Ireland) Regulations 2020 are still to be fully implemented.

The Abortion Act states that an abortion can be carried out if two doctors agree:
> (a) that the pregnancy is less than 24 weeks and that having an abortion would cause less harm to the pregnant woman's physical or mental health or that of any of the existing children of her family, than continuing the pregnancy; or
> (b) that the abortion would prevent grave permanent injury to the physical or mental health of the pregnant woman; or
> (c) that continuing the pregnancy would involve greater risk to the life of the pregnant woman, than if the pregnancy were terminated; or

(d) that there is a substantial risk that if the child were born it would suffer from such physical or mental abnormalities as to be seriously handicapped.[7]

The Abortion (Northern Ireland) Regulations 2020 go further and allow abortion without any reason up to 12 weeks gestation. They state, "A registered medical professional may terminate a pregnancy where a registered medical professional is of the opinion, formed in good faith, that the pregnancy has not exceeded its 12th week."[8]

As a GP who trained in Scotland, I have seen first-hand what the Abortion Act means in practice. When a pregnant lady requests an abortion most doctors will refer her to hospital with very few questions being asked. Safeguards may be spoken about in theory, but generally the reality is that whoever wants an abortion gets one. Unborn children are destroyed simply for being an inconvenience.

Just because the government says it is permissible to have an abortion should not mean that we therefore agree. As Peter states in Acts 5:29, *"We ought to obey God rather than men."* Society's standards will change but God's law does not.

What does an abortion involve?

There are two types of abortion, medical and surgical. Medical abortion involves taking two different medications, one of which blocks a necessary pregnancy hormone (progesterone) while the other causes premature contractions of the womb. This results in the unborn baby being expelled from its mother. Surgical abortion up to 15 weeks gestation involves the unborn baby being removed with a suction tube alone. After 15 weeks it is removed in fragments using a suction tube and forceps.[9]

Abortion, whether medical or surgical, deliberately ends the life of an unborn child. If a person were to pull a baby apart with forceps and suction it would be murder. Yet many try to convince themselves that there is nothing morally repugnant with doing this to a baby in the womb. Babies at risk of being born severely handicapped, despite being able to move, feel pain and even breath on their own, are legally allowed to be torn in pieces from their mother's womb right up to 40 weeks gestation. Convenience has triumphed over conscience.

Deliberately ending the life of an innocent human being is wrong. It breaks the sixth commandment. It is murder regardless of what the law or the doctor may say.

The consequences of abortion for the mother

The effect of abortion on mothers is often underplayed. There are a number of possible short-term complications that mothers may experience, such as bleeding and infection. But it is the long-term consequences I want to focus on.[10]

I have seen many mothers with depression and anxiety that could be linked back to abortions they had when they were younger. The fact that they were responsible for ending the life of their own child will remain with them until the day they die. Sometimes it can be years later before the reality of what they did hits home. Once the abortion has taken place, that little life can never be recovered. All of the potential it had is gone.

The strongest scientific evidence of the negative mental health effects of abortion comes from Professor Priscilla Coleman who conducted a meta-analysis of 22 scientific studies in 2011 (which included a total of 877,181 participants). A meta-analysis is a systematic review that combines the results of multiple

> **There is a clear statistical footprint suggesting elevated risks of mental health problems amongst women having abortions."**

research studies giving a final verdict. It is considered to be the strongest type of scientific evidence. Professor Coleman found higher rates of substance misuse, anxiety, depression and suicidal thoughts among women who had an abortion. In fact, there was an "81% increased risk of mental health problems, and nearly 10% of the incidence of mental health problems was shown to be attributable to abortion."[11]

Many critics have tried to dismiss Coleman's evidence as poorly-conducted research or have accused her of having a pro-life bias. However, Professor David Fergusson, a pro-choice atheist from New Zealand, who has himself conducted research into the link between abortions and mental health problems, writes in relation to Coleman's research:

> *"The implications of this analysis are inescapable: despite the claims made in previous reviews about the absence of association between abortion and mental health, when data are pooled across studies there is consistent evidence suggesting that women having abortions are at modestly increased risks of mental health problems when compared with women coming to term with unplanned/unwanted pregnancies... There is a clear statistical footprint suggesting elevated risks of mental health problems amongst women having abortions."*[12]

Fergusson's own research into a group of 500 females from birth to the age of 30 found that, "abortion was associated with a small increase in the risk of mental disorders; women who had had abortions had rates of mental disorder that were about 30% higher." In his conclusion he makes an important point, which is overlooked by those advocating abortion:

> *"In general, there is no evidence in the literature on abortion and mental health that suggests that abortion reduces the mental health risks of unwanted or mistimed pregnancy."*[13]

The implications of this are important. Approximately 98% of abortions in the UK are on the grounds that it is better for the mother's mental health if she has an abortion than if she continues the pregnancy.[14] However, research and science do not support this idea.[15] Abortion in the majority of cases does not help the mother's mental health. It quite likely harms it.

A possible link with breast cancer?

Some scientific studies have also highlighted another negative effect of abortion: a possible increased risk of breast cancer. A recent meta-analysis published in *Medicine* in 2018 concluded that abortion might increase the risk of breast cancer in women who have already had children. In first time mothers the same effect was not seen.[16]

Another meta-analysis published in 2018 looking at studies on South Asian women showed a moderately strong association between abortion and breast cancer.[17] A further meta-analysis conducted in China in 2014 found a significant association between abortion and increased risk of breast cancer in Chinese females, and interestingly they concluded that the risk of breast cancer increases as the number of abortions increases.[18]

It must be acknowledged that there have been other meta-analyses that conclude there is no association between abortion and breast cancer.[19] More research is needed. Yet the fact that there is some fairly robust evidence of a possible link should be a further reason to question why abortion is promoted so vigorously in our society.

Summary

Although abortion may be common and legal, it is neither beneficial for mother nor baby. There likely are long-term negative consequences for mothers' mental wellbeing, and possible physical consequences too. But, more importantly, abortion ends the lives of millions of babies annually. Abortion is no different from infanticide. It cruelly destroys the life and potential of the unborn. There can be no moral justification for this.

MADE IN HIS IMAGE

CHAPTER 5
ALTERNATIVES TO ABORTION: RESPONDING WITH LOVE

"Be imitators of God as dear children. And walk in love, as Christ also has loved us and given Himself for us, an offering and a sacrifice to God for a sweet-smelling aroma." **Ephesians 5:1-2**

It is essential that, as we respond to the issue of abortion, we are marked by love. Every believer is guilty of breaking God's law and each of us has experienced the blessing of His love, mercy and grace when He saved us and set us free. We know the peace, joy and forgiveness there is in Christ. Therefore we have no right to look down on others or be hard-hearted towards them. Our response to those who have had an abortion, or those with an unplanned pregnancy, must be a visible demonstration of Christ's love. Our heart's desire should be that they too might find our Saviour and the peace and healing He offers.

a) Caring for the unborn
■ *"A bruised reed He will not break."* **Isaiah 42:3**

While most antenatal scans are joyful occasions offering parents the first glimpses of their growing baby, a small number of scans bring the unexpected news that the baby has a problem.

With modern testing techniques a diagnosis can sometimes be confirmed before birth. Some conditions such as anencephaly and Edwards' Syndrome mean the baby will not be able to survive for long outside the womb, and mothers face the distressing prospect of carrying the baby to term, giving birth and then seeing the baby die in the following days or weeks. There are other conditions such as Down's Syndrome that mean the baby will have a close to normal life expectancy but will likely have significant learning difficulties or other health problems.

These unborn babies need cared for as much as any other. Simply because they have health problems does not make them any less valuable, or give us the right to end their lives. The verse above reminds us of the Lord Jesus' care for the damaged and injured. He did not discard or destroy the bruised reed. Nor does He want us to dispose of these little babies because of their disability.

These babies' fragile lives are to be welcomed and valued. Psalm 139:16,17 reminds us that even the *"unformed"* substance of an embryo is known and loved by God.

> *"Your eyes saw my substance, being yet unformed.*
> *And in Your book they all were written,*
> *The days fashioned for me,*
> *When as yet there were none of them.*
> *How precious also are Your thoughts to me, O God!*
> *How great is the sum of them!"*

No matter how long these little ones live they have a value and purpose. Clearly there is tremendous sadness because of the health problems they face and their lack of development. Their untimely death is heart-breaking and will never be forgotten. Yet what joy they can bring and what life lessons they can teach in their short lives.

> **No matter how long these little ones live ... what joy they can bring and what life lessons they can teach in their short lives."**

2 Samuel 12:23 records the occasion when David's first child from Bathsheba died only seven days old. David is recorded as saying, *"I shall go to him, but he shall not return to me,"* which highlights the fact that these little ones have an eternal spirit which will go to be with God forever when they die. How we treat them is of great consequence. They cannot just be cast aside. They are as human as we are.

Mothers of babies with severe life-limiting conditions may be prompted by health professionals to terminate the pregnancy. But life does not always follow what the medical textbooks say. We must remember that doctors cannot tell the future. Even with the most accurate types of investigations there is a small margin of error, and there will always be the possibility of false positives and false negatives. Some babies who doctors thought would be born with a severe disability have not been.[20] Others who were expected to be severely handicapped have been able to have surgery to allow them to lead a relatively normal life.[21] What a tragedy it would have been if they had been aborted.

Some babies who do have a serious genetic problem still live for a few weeks after birth. I recall one baby I met when I was working as a junior doctor on a paediatric ward. He had been born with Edwards' syndrome and had all the typical features: a small head, small jaw and overlapping fingers. We were taught in medical school that this genetic condition is incompatible with life, so I was amazed to see this little one being able to breathe, and being tube-fed on the ward. He lived for just over a month, and his parents were able to bring him home for a few days before he died.

The time his family had with him was so valuable. They were able to hold him, sing to him, dress him and clean him. For those few weeks they were able to love that little one. He was their son. They were so glad they had that time to create such unforgettable memories. This is a much more dignified way to treat an ill baby than ending its life with a suction tube and forceps before it ever sees the light of day.

We must also realise that a lot can be done to help these little lives. Fetal medicine is the branch of medicine that looks after the unborn baby. Babies are able to undergo blood transfusions and a number of other surgical procedures such as shunt placement and cyst drainage while still living in the womb. After birth paediatric surgeons can perform a wide range of life-saving surgeries for otherwise fatal heart, liver and lung conditions. The options for treating these serious congenital conditions are only going to broaden with time. For those with incurable conditions, there is much that palliative care can do to lessen pain and suffering.

Babies deserve the best of treatment, and we as Christians should love and support parents who find themselves in the unexpected situation of having a baby with a life-limiting condition. By providing a listening ear, a freshly cooked meal, getting the shopping or minding the children we can help make an unimaginably difficult time slightly more bearable. Even more importantly we can bring them to our loving God in prayer and intercession.

b) Caring for the mothers involved
◾ *"He has sent Me to heal the brokenhearted."* **Luke 4:18**

The majority of women who have an abortion do so because they feel there is no other feasible option. They feel that continuing the pregnancy would be too much to handle. For many, life feels like it is spiralling out of control and they see nowhere else to turn. If they are to realise that there is a genuine alternative to abortion, they will need loving and consistent support. The first year after childbirth is always difficult even with a supportive husband and mother. For those in crisis, with little family support, raising a child may seem impossible.

In John 8:1-11, when the Lord Jesus was confronted with a woman caught committing adultery, He neither condoned her sin nor condemned her. He pointed out that the men who were accusing her were also guilty of sin and deserved punishment. It was only after doing this that He said to the lady, *"Neither do I condemn you: go and sin no more."* This grace and truth should mark us also, as we interact with broken, hurting women. Their unplanned pregnancies may be a result of sinful choices, but this should not disqualify them from our love and care. We must always remember that God has been gracious and merciful to us. His love needs to be seen in our own attitudes and actions as we seek to care for the broken-hearted just as Christ did.

A lot of agencies offer professional help and support to women.[22] We as individuals will not have the resources to meet all the need that exists. But we do have a responsibility to be present in our communities, building relationships with unbelievers. We should be known as loving believers that can be counted on for support. I know a number of Christian ladies who have been there for single mums in their hour of need. It can be thankless work. The phone-call or message asking for help often comes at the hour it is least wanted; when dinner has just started or just as the children need collected from school. Yet Christ's love was sacrificial and ours should be too.

When we reach out to mothers in need there is always a possibility of being taken advantage of. But it is better to lose a little money and show a lot of love, than to be hard hearted to women in genuine need. Let us not forget that our actions have eternal consequences. Through demonstrating the unconditional love of God, and bringing God's truth into dark, hopeless situations, we may not only save the unborn from abortion, but more importantly we may see souls saved from hell. This is a much-needed ministry.

c) Caring in extremely difficult circumstances

There are very rare instances when a pregnancy may threaten a mother's life. For example, an **ectopic pregnancy** is a pregnancy that develops outside the womb. As it grows it risks tearing the mother's fallopian tubes or other organs, causing catastrophic bleeding. If that were to happen, the mother would die. Both the mother's and baby's rights need to be considered. As both are in danger of death, most Christians would agree that it is morally acceptable to remove the ectopic pregnancy in order to save the mother's life. Rather than both dying, one life is saved.

Those supporting abortion often raise the scenario of a **pregnancy from rape**. The question is posed, "Are you saying that a woman who has been the victim of a horrendous sexual assault now has to carry the child of her attacker for nine months and then give birth to it?" This is a heart-rending scenario. The Bible is clear that rape is wrong and that sex should only take place in the context of a loving marriage (1 Thessalonians 4:3). Yet we must remember that rape leads to only a very small proportion of all pregnancies,[23] and most abortions are for other causes. Pregnancies from rape should not be used as a justification for all abortions.

Women who have been victims of rape need love, support and counselling. In the UK the NHS runs sexual assault centres where victims are offered health screening, counselling and support from police, medics and women's charities. We as Christians also need to be ready and willing to help anyone who experiences such a traumatic event.

But in relation to the matter of abortion, we need to ask whether abortion helps rape victims' healing or does it in fact add further trauma to these already-hurting victims? We have already noted in the previous chapter that there is a lack of scientific evidence proving that abortion helps women's mental health and that it instead will likely have a negative effect on their long-term wellbeing.

It is interesting that Ireland's National Rape Crisis statistics for 2015 showed that 37% of the 53 women who become pregnant following rape went on to give birth and parent their children. Only 24% chose to have an abortion, while 11% chose to put up their child for adoption or fostering. The remaining 28% of babies were miscarried or stillborn.[24] We might think that those who have suffered the horrendous ordeal of rape would not want to raise the baby that is conceived, but the evidence suggests a significant proportion do.[25]

One rape survivor named Liz Carl, who was drugged and raped while still a teenager, said the following, "I no longer care who the biological father is, he is nothing. But look at my son. Just because he was not conceived in an act of love — or a wanted act at all — he is still a precious human being who is deserving of life and everything in it. In fact, I can say that ultimately one thing has saved me from severe, severe depression, and that is my baby. Someone who has been conceived in rape is not less of a person."[26] On another occasion she said, "If I had done what society had told me to do *[i.e. get an abortion]* I would have been robbed of so much joy and so much healing."[27]

We considered the value of human life in Chapter 2 and saw that all human life is of great value, regardless of its age, location or health. This inherent value is not diminished by the fact an unborn child was conceived in horrific, brutal circumstances. Although unwanted, it is a unique human life full of potential. It too is made in God's image and is known and loved by Him. It should not be discarded.

Ken, who was conceived through rape and was adopted at birth, said the following: "I think rape is horrible, but what I want to say to women out there is: you can take something that was terribly done to you, and make something good out of it. And that's, *[voice breaks]* that's me."[28] These little ones are as human and as precious as any other child.

In summary, abortion following rape punishes the unborn child for a crime it did not commit, and risks causing further damage to the mother. It does not remove the trauma of rape and should not be viewed as the obvious answer to such terrible circumstances.

d) Caring for the unwanted

> *"I delivered the poor who cried out, the fatherless and the one who had no helper."* **Job 29:12**

Approximately 98% of abortions are performed due to the fact that the child is not wanted and is considered a "risk to the mother's mental health."[29] Because of this, multitudes of babies' lives are cut short and never reach their potential. Tragically, some children who do survive until birth are also unwanted, facing neglect and sometimes emotional and physical abuse. Children in these situations often end up being looking after by social services, either in foster care or in children's homes. They experience much instability and many of them never know what it is to truly belong in a family. This is not what these children deserve.

The Old Testament character Job was a man of outstanding moral excellence. There was *"none like him on the earth, a blameless and upright man"* (Job 1:8). He was exemplary in his care for the unwanted and vulnerable. He helped the poor, fatherless and helpless in their distress. More than that, he delivered them, standing up to *"the wicked"* that oppressed them (Job 29:17). James 1:27 makes it clear that Christians should follow his example: *"Pure and undefiled religion before God and the Father is this: to visit orphans and widows in their trouble."* We should have a concern for those who are unwanted, or underprivileged. Surely children in state care fall into this category.

One way in which some may have opportunity to help these children is through kinship care, in which extended family members, such as grandparents or an aunt and uncle, look after the child. This can bring a stable, loving influence into the child's life, which is so beneficial to their development. However, each case is different and sometimes there may still be contact with the birth parents, which may have a destabilising effect on the child.

Many children in care are awaiting adoption but there are not enough adoptive parents available to meet this need. In the past 4 years the number of adoptions in England has been falling,[30] despite a yearly rise in the number of children in care. Adoption can totally transform a child's life. In the best-case scenario, they go from being unwanted to being deeply loved and cared for. They receive a new family identity and for the first time in their lives they truly belong. They become full, permanent and legal members of their new family.[31]

Those of us who have been saved by God's grace know the blessing of adoption, for we have been adopted into God's family (Galatians 4:5). At great cost, God rescued us from our hopeless condition, when we were defiled and broken by our sins and had only eternal judgment to look forward to. God placed His Holy Spirit within us and has given us the wonderful prospect of spending eternity in His presence. He has given us an inexhaustible inheritance, making us *"joint heirs with Christ"* (Romans 8:15-17). How amazing it is to be one of His children, and to know His deep and consistent love.

Christians have an opportunity to demonstrate this love in a very real way. Through adopting, fostering or providing kinship care to neglected children, we can play a small part in providing a feasible alternative to mothers who are considering abortion. We should be asking the Lord whether He would have us open our families and homes to one or more of these needy children. In doing so we need to accept the reality that regardless of how we seek to help, life will probably be difficult for these children. Most will carry the emotional scars of their traumatic early years for the rest of their lives.

Although adopting or fostering is not an easy undertaking, we could be a great help to some child, offering them the unconditional love and stable environment they deserve, and ultimately introducing them to the Lord. These precious children could also be a blessing to us, teaching us something of what it cost God to love us, causing us to trust God more deeply and challenging us to grow in Christian grace and love.

Many of us may be unable, at present, to undertake the colossal task of caring for these vulnerable children. But there are other ways we can help. Perhaps we know a family who is involved in fostering, or one who is in the middle of an adoption application.

By supporting them practically them with meals and other necessities, or by showing friendship, we can enable them to fulfil their vital role. Most importantly we can pray for them, for the challenge they face in their calling to love and protect these unwanted children is immense.

e) Caring for the unexpected

> *"'For My thoughts are not your thoughts, nor are your ways My ways', says the Lord. 'For as the heavens are higher than the earth, so are My ways higher than your ways, and My thoughts than your thoughts.'"* **Isaiah 55:8,9**

My wife and I were living in Scotland when our first child was born. Both sets of grandparents were a boat ride away in Ireland, and although the Christians where we lived were so helpful and hospitable, we found raising a child with no family nearby to be quite challenging at times.

By the time our baby boy was three months old we were beginning to settle into a routine. So it was a jaw-dropping discovery to learn that we were expecting again! Number two was due to be born a week before our boy's first birthday. We could hardly believe it. Our very own set of "Irish twins". For many this scenario may have seemed the thing of nightmares, and I know of instances when these exact circumstances have led to an abortion. Yet thanks to God's grace in our lives and the truth of His Word we accepted this unexpected pregnancy for what it was: a gift from God. What a blessing that little life has turned out to be.

Our daughter was born six days before her brother's first birthday, and was home in time for his birthday party. She was just who our family needed. Three years later our toddlers are best friends. It is a joy to hear them running around the house laughing and chatting away to one another. Their vastly different personalities balance each other wonderfully and they have been learning to share long before most others their age. I admit I may be biased, but never have I known such an intelligent, sweet, caring, yet determined little girl. God knew what He was doing when He gave us this gift, and He alone knows the plans He has for her.

Having two babies in such quick succession may have been hard, but we would have it no other way. What a heart-rending tragedy it would be if our daughter were not with us. Yet there are millions of babies' lives cut short by abortion for the sake of convenience or career.

If you are facing an unexpected pregnancy remember that God has a purpose for that little life. It may not have been in your plans, but it has always been in His. There are no unplanned pregnancies with God. We have no right to destroy an irreplaceable, unborn baby, which God has formed in His image and made for His glory. Instead we are called to accept them, love them and raise them to fulfil their potential to the glory of God.

ENDNOTES AND REFERENCES

Chapter 2. The Value of Human Life

[1] Express. Videos. Golden Globes: Michelle Williams addresses abortion in speech. Published Jan 6 2020. Accessed at: https://www.express.co.uk/videos/6119980259001/Golden-Globes-Michelle-Williams-addresses-abortion-in-speech

[2] Chibber KS, Biggs MA, Roberts SC, Foster DG. The role of intimate partners in women's reasons for seeking abortion. *Womens Health Issues*. 2014 Jan-Feb;24(1):e131-8. doi: 10.1016/j.whi.2013.10.007. PMID: 24439939. Accessed at: https://pubmed.ncbi.nlm.nih.gov/24439939/

Chapter 3. At What Point Does Human Life Begin?

[3] Alan Shelmon and Professor Cecili Chadwick. "Should Abortion Be Illegal?" Debate. California State University, San Marcos. 20/04/2010. Accessed at: https://strplace.wordpress.com/2010/04/26/my-abortion-debate/

[4] BBC. Arguments in favour of Abortion. Ethics Guide. Accessed at: http://www.bbc.co.uk/ethics/abortion/mother/for_1.shtml#h3

Chapter 4. The Reality of Abortion

[5] World Health Organisation. Preventing unsafe abortion. 26 June 2019. Accessed at: https://www.who.int/news-room/fact-sheets/detail/preventing-unsafe-abortion

[6] Royal College of Obstetricians & Gynaecologists. Information for you. Abortion Care. February 2012. Accessed at: https://www.rcog.org.uk/globalassets/documents/patients/patient-information-leaflets/pregnancy/pi-abortion-care.pdf

[7] Abortion Act 1967 Section 1 Medical termination of pregnancy. Accessed at: http://www.legislation.gov.uk/ukpga/1967/87/section/1

[8] The Abortion (Northern Ireland) Regulations 2020 Part 2 Grounds for termination: cases with gestational limit. Accessed at: https://www.legislation.gov.uk/uksi/2020/345/part/2/chapter/1/made

[9] Royal College of Obstetricians & Gynaecologists. Information for you. Abortion Care. February 2012. Accessed at: https://www.rcog.org.uk/globalassets/documents/patients/patient-information-leaflets/pregnancy/pi-abortion-care.pdf

[10] A very helpful summary entitled "Abortion: risks and complications" has been produced by the Christian Medical Fellowship. Accessible at: http://admin.cmf.org.uk/pdf/publicpolicy/abortion-briefing-paper-2015.pdf

[11] Coleman, P. (2011). Abortion and mental health: Quantitative synthesis and analysis of research published 1995–2009. *British Journal of Psychiatry*, 199(3), 180-186. doi:10.1192/bjp.bp.110.077230

[12] Saunders P. David Fergusson wades in to defend Coleman over abortion mental health link. National Right to Life News 20 October 2011. bit.ly/2CQszg7

[13] Fergusson, D., Horwood, L., & Boden, J. (2008). Abortion and mental health disorders: Evidence from a 30-year longitudinal study. *British Journal of Psychiatry*, 193(6), 444-451. doi:10.1192/bjp.bp.108.056499

[14] Department of Health and Social Care. Abortion Statistics, England and Wales: 2019. Summary information from the abortion notification forms returned to the Chief Medical Officers of England and Wales. January to December 2019. P10. Accessed at: https://assets.publishing.service.gov.uk/government/uploads/system/uploads/attachment_data/file/891405/abortion-statistics-commentary-2019.pdf

[15] Further evidence of adverse mental health effects have been described by Pedersen. In a study of 768 women he concluded that, "young adult women who undergo induced abortion may be at increased risk for subsequent depression." [Pedersen, W. (2008). Abortion and depression: A population-based longitudinal study of young women. *Scandinavian Journal of Public Health*, 36(4), 424–428. https://doi.org/10.1177/1403494807088449]

[16] Deng, Yongchun MD; Xu, Hua MM; Zeng, XiaoHua MD* Induced abortion and breast cancer, *Medicine*: January 2018 - Volume 97 - Issue 3 - p e9613 doi: 10.1097/MD.0000000000009613

[17] Brind J, Condly SJ, Lanfranchi A, Rooney B. Induced abortion as an independent risk factor for breast cancer: a systematic review and meta-analysis of studies on south asian women. *Issues Law Med*. Spring 2018;33(1):32-54.

[18] Huang Y, Zhang X, Li W, et al. A meta-analysis of the association between induced abortion and breast cancer risk among Chinese females. *Cancer Causes & Control* : CCC. 2014 Feb;25(2):227-236. DOI: 10.1007/s10552-013-0325-7.

[19] Guo, J., Huang, Y., Yang, L. et al. Association between abortion and breast cancer: an updated systematic review and meta-analysis based on prospective studies. *Cancer Causes & Control* (2015) 26, 811–819. https://doi.org/10.1007/s10552-015-0536-1

[20] Kidszun et al. What If the Prenatal Diagnosis of a Lethal Anomaly Turns Out to Be Wrong? *Pediatrics* May 2016, 137 (5) e20154514; DOI: 10.1542/peds.2015-4514 Accessed at: https://pediatrics.aappublications.org/content/137/5/e20154514

[21] Right to Life. UK mother told to have abortion 10 times after baby found to have disability. June 6, 2019. Accessed at: https://righttolife.org.uk/news/uk-mother-told-to-have-abortion-10-times-after-baby-found-to-have-disability/

Chapter 5. Alternatives to Abortion: Responding with Love

[22] I would suggest signposting mothers and families with a crisis pregnancy to PregnancyMatters (pregnancymatters.org.uk, National helpline: 0808 802 5433) although there are likely other support agencies available in your area. PregnancyMatters is a UK wide, pro-life charity that provides counselling, and emotional support, as well as practical support such as baby equipment, training in parenting skills and housing for vulnerable mothers.

[23] Data from the Republic of Ireland in 2015 recorded only 5% of rape victims becoming pregnant. (Rape Crisis Network Ireland. National Rape Crisis Statistics 2015. Available at https://www.rcni.ie/wp-content/uploads/RCNI-RCC-StatsAR-2015-1.pdf)

[24] Rape Crisis Network Ireland. National Rape Crisis Statistics 2015. Available at https://www.rcni.ie/wp-content/uploads/RCNI-RCC-StatsAR-2015-1.pdf

[25] Another study of pregnancies from rape showed 32.2% of women kept the baby. (Holmes MM, Resnick HS, Kilpatrick DG, Best CL. Rape-related pregnancy: estimates and descriptive characteristics from a national sample of women. *Am J Obstet Gynecol*. 1996 Aug;175(2):320-4; discussion 324-5. doi: 10.1016/s0002-9378(96)70141-2. PMID: 8765248.) Accessed at: https://pubmed.ncbi.nlm.nih.gov/8765248/

[26] Quotation from Liz Carl accessed at: http://cdn.thejournal.ie/media/2016/11/life-canvass-book-landscape-update-lo-res-nov-16-single-pages-1.pdf

ENDNOTES AND REFERENCES

[27] Liz Carl video accessed at: https://www.youtube.com/watch?v=-bRvWYMjlj4

[28] Ken's story accessed at: https://www.lifenews.com/2012/09/11/kens-story-i-was-conceived-in-rape-dont-kill-me-in-abortion/

[29] Department of Health and Social Care. Abortion Statistics, England and Wales: 2019. Summary information from the abortion notification forms returned to the Chief Medical Officers of England and Wales. January to December 2019. P10. Accessed at: https://assets.publishing.service.gov.uk/government/uploads/system/uploads/attachment_data/file/891405/abortion-statistics-commentary-2019.pdf

[30] National Statistics, Department of Education. Children looked after in England (including adoption), year ending 31 December 2019. Accessed at: https://assets.publishing.service.gov.uk/government/uploads/system/uploads/attachment_data/file/850306/Children_looked_after_in_England_2019_Text.pdf

[31] Adoption UK. What is Adoption? Accessed at: https://www.adoptionuk.org/about-modern-adoption